WALK BORROW[ ]
& KES[ ]

TWENTY WALKS [ ]
SEATHWAITE, SEATOL[ ] [ ]VAITE,
THORNTHWAITE, ROSTH[ ] [ ]ATENDLATH,
GRANGE, LODORE, NEWLA[ ] [ ], DERWENTWATER,
KESWICK, BRAITHWAITE & BASSENTHWAITE

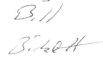

BY BILL BIRKETT

BB

BILL BIRKETT PUBLISHING

PUBLISHED BY BILL BIRKETT PUBLISHING

This book is dedicated to the many friends who insisted on its completion. I would particularly like to thank Andrew and Jeremy Sheehan, for joining me on many a Borrowdale adventure, Anne Corrie, who wouldn't listen to my excuses and Emma and Tobias for enthusiasm and website.

Cover photograph: Over Derwentwater from Surprise View in early Spring.
Backcover photographs: The Bowderstone - Walk 8, Castlerigg - Walk 17, Derwentwater - Walk 12, Seathwaite - Walks 1/2/3 & 4.
Page [i] photograph: South over Derwentwater to The Jaws of Borrowdale with the Scafell Massif beyond.

All photographs from the Bill Birkett Photo Library
Maps by Martin Bagness based on pre-1950 Ordnance Survey maps. Completely redrawn 2013.

First published in the UK in 2014
Copyright © Bill Birkett 2014

A catalogue record for this book is available from The British Library

ISBN 978-0-9564296-3-6

Book Design by Bill Birkett
Proof Read by Claire Willett, Jeremy Sheehan & Denis Bland
Printed in Bowness by Badger Press (www.badgerpress.co.uk)
for Bill Birkett Publishing
www.billbirkett.co.uk
Dale View, Little Langdale, Cumbria, LA22 9NY

DISCLAIMER

Walking in the country and over the fells is potentially dangerous activity and each individual following the routes described within this book is responsible for their own safety and actions. Neither the author nor the publisher accepts any responsibility for the individual safety or actions of anyone using this book. Although the author encountered no difficulty of access on the routes described, and while considerable effort has been made to avoid so doing, the inclusion of a route does not imply that a right of way or right of access exists in every case or in all circumstances. Readers are also advised that changes can occur to the landscape that may affect the contents of this book. The author welcomes notification of any such changes.

Tel:
015394 37272

email:
olddungeonghyll1@btconnect.com

www.odg.co.uk

A Real Escape
No TV. No Radio. No Newspapers. One of the last places in the Lake District where you can relax with real peace and tranquillity

The Old Dungeon Ghyll Hotel

A unique hotel situated in the remote and unspoilt Langdale Valley

Our Hotel and Famous Climbers/Hikers Bar offer Homemade food and a selection of real ales

Lunch time Bar Meals served from 12 noon to 2pm
Evening Bar Meals served from 6pm to 9pm

Wi-fi is available if essential ✿ We are Child & Dog Friendly

The hotel is accessible on public transport via a bus from Ambleside

[iii]

CONTENTS

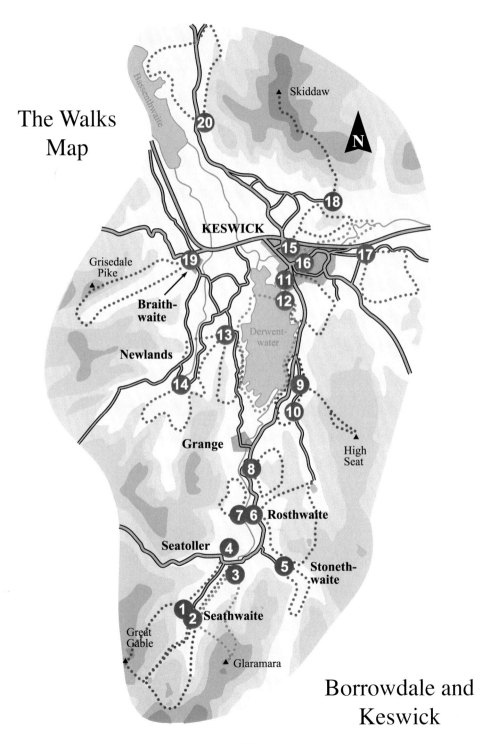

The Walks Map

Skiddaw

N

KESWICK

Grisedale Pike

Braith-waite

Newlands

Derwent-water

Grange

High Seat

Rosthwaite

Seatoller

Stoneth-waite

Seathwaite

Great Gable

Glaramara

Borrowdale and Keswick

INTRODUCTION – WALK BORROWDALE AND KESWICK

Perfect for walking, there is no more completely beautiful valley than Borrowdale. Surrounded by shapely fells, it runs for some 9 miles from its twin heads of Seathwaite and Langstrath, via open meadow and broad leaved woods and stone built villages, squeezing through The Jaws of Borrowdale to open over magnificent Derwentwater, finally to reach the historic town of Keswick. A myriad world of fell, crag, wood, waterfall, tarn, quarry, mine, farm and lake. You could take many lifetimes to appreciate its complexities. It has a richness of detail, extreme of form and contrast of mood that are unequalled. Yet, like few other places in the world of comparable quality, it is open and accessible. On the high tops freedom to roam is unrestricted, on the lower heights and in the valleys there are many paths, tracks and byways.

From many places within the valley you can look to all three of Lakeland's mountain massifs over 3,000ft. Scafell and Great Gable stand to the south and Skiddaw to the north, Glaramara to the east and Catbells and Grisedale Pike to the west. Below the heights the valley and lower slopes have stunning variety. The emptiness of Langstrath, closely resembling a remote Scottish Glen, contrasts with the sylvan beauty of Seathwaite before both merge to widen into the open meadows around Rosthwaite. Then, heading northwards, the valley closes to enter the rocky Jaws of Borrowdale, fiercely guarded by Castle Crag, before opening once again to reveal the oak bejewelled shores of the resplendent Derwentwater lake. Secretive side valleys and hanging basins, particularly those of Watendlath, Newlands and Gillercombe, provide further intrigue and mystery before, finally, Keswick will be found nestling at the foot of mighty Skiddaw. Here the Greta, rushing through its gorge, and the Derwent, meet to flow into the head of Bassenthwaite Lake watched over by the pyramidal Grisedale Pike.

Yet there is so much of intrinsic interest here that you could easily dismiss the exceptional beauty of the area and emerge yourself in the detail:- The flora and fauna, so many species of tree and plant. The historical interest with The Neolithic Stone Axe Factory on Glaramara, the Bronze Age Castlerigg Stone Circle and ancient hill fort atop Castle Crag. The human interest from the farming of the famous Herdwick Fell Sheep, to the ancient mines, for gold, copper, cobalt, graphite and the quarrying of the exquisite light green slate, to the traditional clinker build boats, which still ply the surface of the lake angling for Arctic Char. The diverse geology which shape the landforms from the hard Borrowdale Volcanics to the softer, fossil bearing Skiddaw Slates.

I have selected twenty circular walks for this guidebook. They walk the heights, the intermediate and low fells, the valleys and some also start in the little town of Keswick. I have chosen them to take you through the varied world that is Borrowdale and to offer you a range of experiences. Indeed Derwentwater is one of the few great lakes in Britain that you can actually walk most of the way around without being blocked by private land or busy roads. A sublime outing that can be shortened at any stage by simply hopping onto a Keswick Motor Launch should circumstances or offspring dictate. Furthermore, there are many excellent inns, cafes and places of rest on or nearby all these walks.

There is plenty here for everyone, whether you are an experienced fell walker wishing to scale the heights or simply wish to choose to enjoy the delights of the valley. There are walks and experiences here for all seasons and most weather conditions and by perusing the Fact Sheet, which accompanies each walk description, you can easily select a walk to suit.

The format of this guide is simple and straightforward. **Overall maps**, on the back cover and within the contents page (page v), show immediately where the individual walks lie. Each **numbered walk** is described on a double page spread, you don't need to turn the page mid walk, with a suitably **detailed map** that can form the basis of the walk (although it is recommended that you also take an OS map with you for detailed reference and navigation particularly on the high fells). My **photographs** illustrate some highlights and capture the general ambiance of the walk. The **Fact Sheet** provides the essential information and identifies places to eat, drink, rest, shelter on each individual walk. New to this guidebook, colour coded on the **Contents Page,** are **classification** of the walks as; Valley (0 to 200m in altitude), Low Fell (200m to 300m), Intermediate Fell (300m to 700m), High Fell (700m to 1000m). The **ringbinding** keeps the guidebook flat in your pocket and always allows it to open on the page of your chosen walk. Selected adverts provide information on local facilities that I can personally recommend.

Following the immense popularity of "Walk The Langdales", which has been reprinted three times to date, "Walk Ambleside, Rydal and Grasmere", due to be reprinted, and "Walk Windermere and Hawkshead", this is the fourth guidebook in the series published by **Bill Birkett Publishing.** Next in the series, coming soon, is "Walk The Ullswater Area". The books are available both locally and nationally through various outlets and bookshops and signed copies are available directly from my website www.billbirkett.co.uk (postage free in the UK).

CAUTION

Particularly on the fells it is important that walkers have equipment appropriate to both prevailing and possible conditions. Suitable footwear, weatherproof clothing, map and compass or GPS, are essential requirements. Watch to each step. For guidance on navigation, clothing and footwear in both summer and winter, survival and tips on digital photography, see "The Hillwalker's Manual" by Bill Birkett.

WALK 1
TO GREAT GABLE VIA SOURMILK GILL

A wonderful high fell outing climbing to Lakeland's most iconic mountain – Great Gable. The route ascends via Sourmilk Gill and Gillercombe to top Green Gable before crossing Windy Gap to Great Gable. Descent is made down the south east shoulder to Styhead to continue by Styhead Tarn before descending to Stockley Bridge and following the track back to Seathwaite.

THE ROUTE

In the farmyard turn right under the arch. Take the lane between walls to the footbridge which crosses the beck above its confluence with Sourmilk Gill. Take the stile over the wall and ascend by the left side of the gill and its tumbling waterfalls. Finally bear left to a gap in the fell wall.

◆ The path traverses through the barren hanging basin of Gillercombe before rising to the grassy shoulder of Base Brown. Bear right and ascend to the stony summit of Green Gable.

◆ Take the stony drop to Windy Gap and climb steeply up rock

and scree to cross the summit plateau and reach the topmost rocks of Great Gable. A mountain of statue and grace from wherever it is viewed.

◆ A well worn path heads off to Sty Head down the broad south eastern

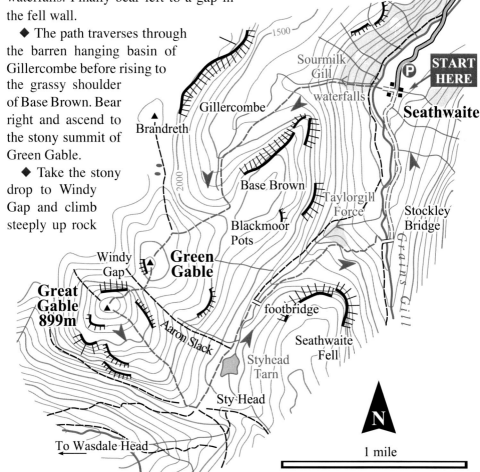

WALK 1

Great Gable and Styhead Tarn, right, viewed from the Scafell Massif

edge of the mountain. Stone steps, scree and rock though nowhere any difficulty. At the col of Styhead bear left to take the distinct path past Styhead Tarn until a footbridge crosses the beck and the path/track leads down the right side of the gill.

Sourmilk Gill

◆ Continue descending the well worn path/ track passing the pines of Greenhow Knott and down to the fell wall. Go through the gate and

continue to a second wall and gate by the stone arch of Stockley Bridge. Beyond the bridge bear left and follow the track back to Seathwaite.

FACT SHEET
CLASS: *High Fell Walk (alt 899m).*
LENGTH: 8 km.
TIME: 4½ hours.
DIFFICULTY: Very difficult, a mountain route with 870m of ascent. Generally the going is rough and stony though there are no technical difficulties.
START & FINISH: The head of the Seathwaite Valley, by the side of the road beneath the farm – don't block any field entrances or the road (237 123).
MAPS: OS L90 or OL4.
HOSTELRIES: Café at the end of Seathwaite farmyard.

WALK 2
SEATHWAITE TO STYHEAD AND SPRINKLING TARNS VIA TAYLORGILL FORCE

A walk into a wonderfully wild mountain world passing one of Lakeland's most spectacular waterfalls and two of its most sublime mountain tarns. There is a short scrambly section to pass the waterfall but the rest of the route is over much travelled stony paths. Leave Seathwaite and ascend to Styhead Tarn to climb once again to pass Sprinkling Tarn. Beyond the tarn fork left, under the shadow of Great End, and make descent by Grains Gill before crossing Stockley Bridge to return along the track to Seathwaite.

THE ROUTE

In the farmyard turn right under the arch. Take the lane between walls to the footbridge which crosses the beck above its confluence with Sourmilk Gill. Immediately go left, taking the little gate through the stone wall. Follow the path which rises through the fields above the west bank of the beck. As the going steepens scrambly ascent leads to a little gate, beyond which there is a view across to Taylorgill Force. The waterfall, particularly impressive in times of spate, falls clear for some 30m down the ravine of Styhead Gill.

◆ Beyond the gate the path rises with a little exposed section of rocky scrambling before continuing more easily. Pass the pines and proceed by the delightful open banks and rock slides of Styhead Gill. The going levels to pass the archetypal mountain tarn - Styhead Tarn.

◆ Above the tarn a path bears left and ascends to pass Sprinkling Tarn. Continue for another 500m until a fork to the left is taken to cross Ruddy Gill. Follow the path down the right side of the gill, now known as Grains Gill, and descend the steep shoulder down the stone steps before crossing the gill and continuing to Stockley

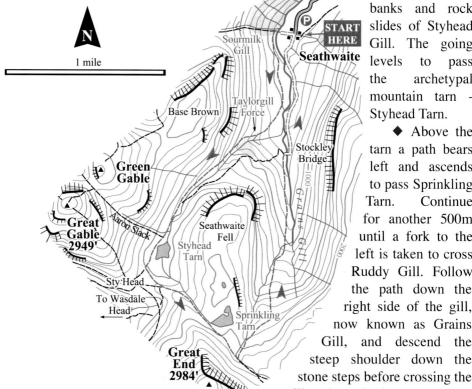

WALK 2

Over Styhead Tarn to Styhead

Sprinkling Tarn with Great Gable beyond

Bridge. Cross the bridge then bear left
to follow the track back to Seathwaite.

Taylorgill Force

FACT SHEET
CLASS: Intermediate Fell Walk (alt 630m)
LENGTH: 8 km.
TIME: 3½ hours.
*DIFFICULTY: Difficult, with a short
section of rocky scrambling to pass the
waterfall but otherwise on straightforward
paths (500m of ascent).*
*START & FINISH: The head of the
Seathwaite Valley, by the side of the road
beneath the farm – don't block any field
entrances or the road (237123).*
MAPS: OS L90 or OL4 & OL6.
*HOSTELRIES: Café at the end of
Seathwaite farmyard.*

WALK 3
GLARAMARA BY THORNYTHWAITE FELL

Glaramara is the evocatively named high point of the shoulder running between the valleys of Langstrath to the east and Seathwaite to the west. Its most visible feature, seen from the Borrowdale road at the head of the valley, is the great hanging glacial basin known as The Combe. This route climbs the spur forming the right side of The Combe, Thornythwaite Fell, to reach the summit rocks before making a steep descent by the side of Hind Gill to Seathwaite.

FACT SHEET
CLASS: High Fell Walk (alt 783m).
LENGTH: 8¾ km.
TIME: 3½ hours.
DIFFICULTY: Very Difficult, gradual ascent (700m) with a short section of rocky scrambling to gain the summit (can be avoided), very steep descent.
START & FINISH: Wide grassy verge beside the Thornythwaite track (250135) some 100m from Strands Bridge.
MAPS: OS L90 or OL4.
HOSTELRIES: Cafés at Seathwaite and Seatoller.

The Combe with Thornythwaite Fell, right, leading to the top of Glaramara

THE ROUTE
Opposite the parking area there is a gate and wooden stile leading to a stony path. The path rises to turn rightwards to climb through the trees. A kissing gate leads through the stone wall to follow the path ascending into the base of The Combe with the stream of Combe Gill down below. Continue until the way forks then bear right making steep ascent continuing to gain the crest of the ridge of Thornythwaite Fell. Follow the obvious path to traverse the cairned rocky knoll top of Thornythwaite Fell after which the going eases. Keep along

WALK 3

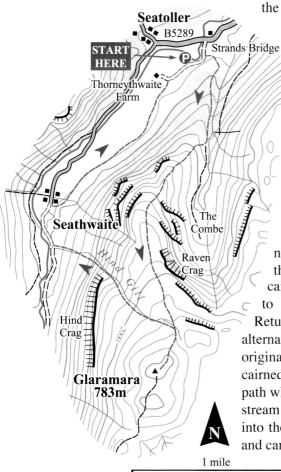

Seatoller
B5289
START HERE
Strands Bridge
Thorneythwaite Farm
Seathwaite
The Combe
Raven Crag
Hind Crag
Glaramara 783m
N
1 mile

Middle top of Glaramara

the shoulder until the way splits again.

◆ Bear right aiming for the twin topped rocky dome which marks the northern end of Glaramara. On arrival a rocky rift splits the crag and this is usually ascended directly (alternatively easier ground lies a short distance over to the right side of the rocky dome).

There are cairns on the knoll to the left and higher knoll to the right. Expansive views to the north. A little way beyond, along the shoulder, there is another cairned rocky top which looks to Great End and Great Gable. Return to descend the rift (or easier alternative) to regain and follow the original path for a short way until a cairned path bears off left. Follow the path which descends to the south of the stream of Hind Gill. As the path moves into the ravine of Hind Gill it steepens and care must be exercised.

◆ Pass through the narrow gap in the wall below the ravine and descend to eventually bear right over the bouldery stream to gain a narrow gate at the right side of the enclosure. Pass through the gate and gain the main track leading to Seathwaite. Go right along the level track and bear right before the buildings to find the path leading beside the meadows back to the Thornythwaite track and starting point.

WALK 4
SEATOLLER TO SEATHWAITE AT THE HEAD OF BORROWDALE

The flat green valley of Seathwaite, running between the hamlets of Seatoller and Seathwaite, forms the most southerly head of Borrowdale. It provides a gateway to the high fells and a number of important mountain passes and contains much of scenic and historical interest. This easy circular route, through a world fossilised in time, traverses the valley floor to pass Folly Bridge, the working hill farm of Seathwaite, the waterfall of Sourmilk Gill, the old Wad Mines, the ancient Borrowdale Yews and Seathwaite Bridge.

THE ROUTE

A path leaves the back of the car park to cross a stile. Bear right and continue above the wall with the interesting building of Glaramara below. Keep along through the large oaks until, at the end of the wall, the path descends to cross Folly Bridge. A slate headstone dates the bridge 1781 and is inscribed; 'I count this folly you have done, as you have neither wife nor son, daughter I have god give her grace, and heaven for her resting place'.

◆ Cross the field to pass the end of Mountain View Cottages and cross the road beneath the hump-backed Strands Bridge, to take the lane opposite. Follow by the river then continue along the track. Bear left at the point where the track swings right to Thorneythwaite Farm. Easy going leads along the south side of the valley to the hamlet of Seathwaite.

◆ Turn right and take the far cobbled lane between the buildings and then left to pass beneath a flat arch leading through the barn. Follow the lane to cross the bridge over the river beneath

the waterfalls of Sourmilk Gill. Go right to cross the little gill by a further footbridge and continue down the northern side of the valley. Above to the left you can just discern the spoil heaps of the old Wad Mines. Worked for over 400 years Seathwaite Wad was once the only source of quality graphite in Europe – worth more than gold, it was protected by armed guards.

◆ In 300 metres the much celebrated Borrowdale Yews stand just above the path to the left. Rather storm damaged and with hollow trunk, the oldest of these trees is thought to be in excess of

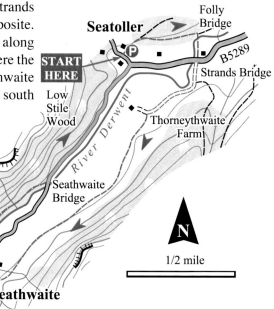

Seathwaite Head amongst the fells

a thousand years in age. Join the road by Seathwaite Bridge and continue left down the road to cross Seatoller Bridge to turn left at the junction.

Seathwaite Farm

Ancient hollow Borowdale Yew

FACT SHEET
CLASS: Valley Walk (alt 125m).
LENGTH: 5½ km.
TIME: 2 hours.
DIFFICULTY: Easy, mainly level going with a short road section.
START & FINISH: Seatoller car park (245 138).
MAPS: OS L90 or OL4.
HOSTELRIES: Cafés at Seatoller and Seathwaite.

WALK 5
STONETHWAITE TO LOWER LANGSTRATH (AND POSSIBLE EXTENSION AROUND UPPER LANGSTRATH)

Flowing between high fells and below rocky crags, through the stark openness of Langstrath and by the oaks of Stonethwaite, the tumbling clear waters of the Stonethwaite and Langstrath Becks are quite magical. In Old Norse (Viking) 'Thwaite' means clearing and 'Lang'; long. 'Strath' is Celtic for river valley. People have loved this quiet place for eons of time. The shorter route crosses the footbridge at Johnny House whilst the longer continues up Langstrath to the foot of Stake Pass before making return.

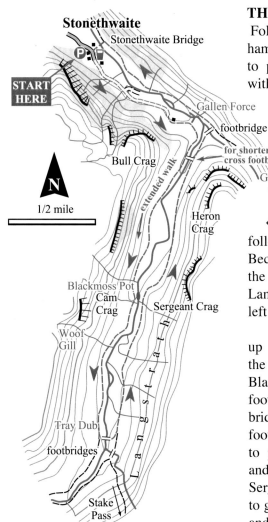

THE ROUTE

Follow the lane through the heart of the hamlet and keep along the stony track to pass Alisongrass Hoghouse woods with the river and campsite down below to the left. Pass a converted stone barn and continue along the walled lane until, at a polished boulder, open ground lies to the left. More interestingly a path leads by the riverside to this same point.

◆ Bear right to the stone lane and follow the west bank of Langstrath Beck. Ascend the walled track to start the long wild, mountain valley of Langstrath. For the shorter route bear left over Johnny House footbridge.

◆ For the longer route continue up the valley of Langstrath, passing the favourite swimming location of Blackmoss Pot, to a footbridge near the foot of the nose of Stake Pass. Cross the bridge and bear left to follow the stony footpath along the east side of the valley to pass beneath Sergeant Crag Slabs and the huge boulder of Gash Rock, Sergeant Crag and finally Heron Crag, to gain Johnny House footbridge. Long and short routes combine once again at this point.

◆ Follow the path along the east bank of the beck walking downstream.

Looking to Stonethwaite and Eagle Crag

Looking down upper Langstrath

Johnny House Footbridge

With the bastion of Eagle Crag above, cross the little wooden footbridge over Greenup Gill to intercept a track. Go left, with the waterfall of Gallen Force amongst the trees down to the left. Continue by wood and field until, opposite Stonethwaite, a little lane leads left over the stone arched Stonethwaite Bridge to regain the hamlet.

FACT SHEET
CLASS: *Valley Walk (alt 220m on ext).*
LENGTH: 4 km (10 km with ext).
TIME: 1½ hours (3 ½ hours with ext).
DIFFICULTY: Easy, mainly level going, though Langstrath is remote.
START & FINISH: Stonethwaite (262 137).
MAPS: OS L89 or OL4.
HOSTELRIES: Café and Langstrath Country Inn in Stonethwaite.

WALK 6
ROSTHWAITE TO WATENDLATH AND DOCK TARN

Contrasting the remote wildness of Watendlath and Dock Tarn with the sylvan beauty of the Borrowdale valley this is a very fine outing indeed. Weather permitting this walk is suitable for most times of the year but is arguably at its finest in late spring, when the lambs gamble and May blossom blooms, or early summertime when Dock Tarn is white with water lilies.

THE ROUTE

Gain the main Borrowdale Road. Go left for a few metres then take the surfaced lane on the right. Cross the stone arch Rosthwaite Bridge. Bear left and ascend the narrow lane then cross a raised walkway to the gate. Continue to ascend the stony track, through the open mixed woods. Beyond the gate in the wall ascend the steep track. Keep right at the junction to pass the stand of Scots Pine and climb to the top of Puddingstone Bank. Traverse the top of the hill and then make the increasingly stony descent to the hamlet of Watendlath.

◆ Just before the water's edge and the hamlet take the track leading off to the right. (However, those wishing

FACT SHEET
CLASS: Intermediate Fell Walk
(alt 420m).
LENGTH: 8.5 km.
TIME: 4 hours.
DIFFICULTY: Mildly difficult, with steepish ascent (500m) and descent.
START & FINISH: Car parks in Rosthwaite (256 149)
MAPS: OS L89 or OL4.
HOSTELRIES: The Flock-in Tearoom and Scafell Hotel in Rosthwaite. Caffle House Tearoom in Watendlath.

to visit the hamlet and tearoom before continuing should cross the narrow packhorse bridge before making return to this point). Follow the lane which opens into a field and continue to ascend

Watendlath

WALK 6

the well defined track. Circumnavigate a bog keeping along the path to its left. At a junction of ways keep left to gain a kissing gate followed by stone steps which climb towards the basin of

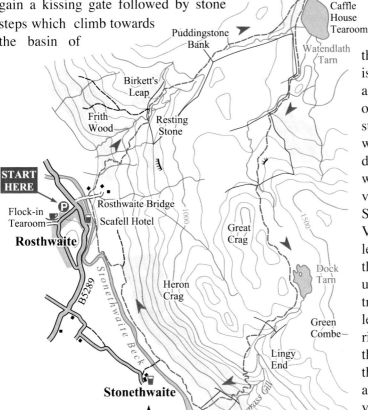

Dock Tarn. Follow the narrow stone path which traverses above the shore of the tarn.

◆ Beyond the tarn the path is well defined and leads down over a wooden stile through the wall and winds down to Ling End with impressive views over the Stonethwaite Valley. Stone steps lead down through the wood. Continue until beyond the trees the path leads diagonally rightwards down the open field. As the going levels at the base of the valley a stony track is intercepted. Bear right along the track, passing the turn-off to the hamlet of Stonethwaite, to a fork. Go left, skirting the elbow in Stonethwaite Beck, and continue along the lane back to Rosthwaite Bridge.

N

1/2 mile

Dock Tarn

Dock Tarn
White Water
Lilies

WALK 7
CASTLE CRAG FROM ROSTHWAITE

Within the 'Jaws of Borrowdale' the ancient hill fort of Castle Crag rises from sylvan splendour and the crystal clear waters of the River Derwent to take commanding position over beautiful Borrowdale. With an option to visit Millican Dalton's 'Cave Hotel' this route circumnavigates the craggy outcrop before ascending to the summit.

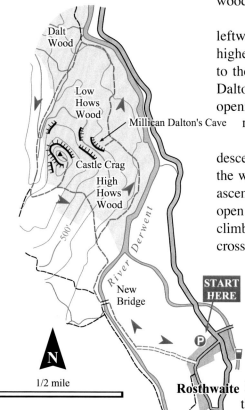

woods of High Hows.

◆ Follow the signed track to rise leftwards through the woods. Near the highest point a narrow path climbs up to the left and this ascends to Millican Dalton's Cave – the highest slate quarry opening. If this is done return to the main track.

◆ Take the track to make stony descent to the riverside. Continue through the woods of Low Hows to make slight ascent to a gate. Beyond this, above the open bend in the river, a track breaks off climbing to the left. Ascend this track to cross a tiny footbridge and rise to quit the wood via a gate. The stone track and rocky steps traverse beneath the steep west face of the crag before a cairn marks a path branching off to the left.

◆ Rise with this path, climbing the west flank of the hill until a ladder stile leads by Scots Pine onto the slate quarry bank. Trend right to ascend the zigzag path up the slate waste to gain the level south shoulder of Castle Crag. Expansive view south over upper Borrowdale. Climb the nose following the zigzag path until a quarry opens on the left. Take the worn path ascending through larch to the right of this. Care, the edges of the quarry are unfenced. Emerge onto the level summit plateau. Observe magnificent aspect over Derwent Water to mighty Skiddaw and the ancient earthwork

THE ROUTE

Bear right along the road past Rosthwaite Village Hall, until a cobbled track leads right through the stone buildings onto a lane. Continue along the lane to meet the tree lined River Dewent. Follow along the river bank before crossing the stone arch of New Bridge. Follow the west bank of the river to pass a rocky knoll bedecked with fine oaks. Keep along the track to make slight ascent before entering the lovely mixed deciduous

WALK 7

Castle Crag rising
beyond New Bridge

Scots Pine
on Castle
Crag

Castle Crag above
the River Derwent

Castle Crag Summit

mound running around the summit rim. The summit lies atop the rocky knoll adorned with commemorative plaque.

◆ Retrace steps to the south shoulder and bear left to find a ladder stile leading south over the stone wall. Bear left and follow the steepening path down the east flank before continuing through woods to regain the original track. Go right, descend to the river, and follow the route back to Rosthwaite.

FACT SHEET
CLASS: Low Fell Walk (alt 290m).
LENGTH: 6 km.
TIME: 2 hours.
DIFFICULTY: Difficult, strenuous ascent (290m) and descent.
START & FINISH: Car parks in Rosthwaite (256 149)
MAPS: OS L89 or OL4.
HOSTELRIES: The Flock-in Tearoom and Scafell Hotel in Rosthwaite.

WALK 8
KING'S HOW AND THE BOWDERSTONE

The heather clad top of King's How overlooks Grange village and the "Jaws of Borrowdale" to offer revealing views north over Derwentwater to Skiddaw and south over Rosthwaite to the Borrowdale Fells. With a rich mixture of impressive rock architecture and natural woodland its ascent skirts the head of Troutdale before return passes by the huge and famous Bowderstone.

THE ROUTE

From the top-most corner of The Bowderstone car park take the stile over the wire fence. A well defined path crosses a small stream and proceeds gently at first to pass some old quarry workings, before a steady pull reaches an open shoulder. To the right lies **START HERE** a distinctive boulder. Above this a sheer rock face, Great End Crag, forms the Borrowdale face of our objective - King's How. On the opposite side of the Troutdale Valley, below, looms the huge precipice of Black Crag – a favourite haunt for rock climbers.

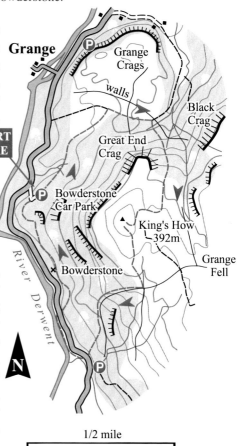

◆ Dropping from the shoulder through the stone wall, the path enters the thickly wooded head of Troutdale. Bearing right, it soon begins to climb steeply through the trees - via stone steps - to emerge onto an open shoulder. From here continue to a wire fence then bear right. Climb to pass the end of a small boggy corridor lying between rocky hummocks. A yew tree on the left marks the way as the path contours around the hillside, moving over rightwards to the Borrowdale face of the fell. In a short way the path makes zigzag ascent through the heather, and continues until it passes a slate plaque (which reads, 'In Loving Memory of King Edward VII Grange Fell is dedicated by his Sister Louise'). A few more metres of ascent gains the summit cairn of King's How.

◆ Descend the path heading south towards Borrowdale and continue down the fellside to a stone wall. Bear right and traverse above the wall until it turns leftwards. Follow the path down the hillside to the right of the wall and cross the wooded Red Brow to gain access to a small parking area by the roadside. Go right and follow the road,

WALK 8

King's How, left, standing above the head of Derwentwater

The heathery summit of King's How

The Bowderstone

a path runs along its left side, until in 450 metres, a small gate stands to the right. Pass through the gate and climb the stony lane to gain the impressively large Bowderstone. Continue along the lane which leads back to the foot of the car park.

FACT SHEET
CLASS: *Intermediate Fell Walk*
(alt 392m).
LENGTH: *4 km.*
TIME: *2 hours.*
DIFFICULTY: *Difficult, strenuous ascent (370m) and descent.*
START & FINISH: *Bowderstone Car Park (253 168).*
MAPS: *OS L89 or OL4.*
HOSTELRIES: *Tearooms and cafés in nearby Grange.*

WALK 9
ASHNESS FELL AND HIGH SEAT

Passing just above the picturesque Ashness Bridge this walk leads from the closed wooded world of Borrowdale to make steep ascent to the open and heather clad heights which define its eastern rim. The rocky summits of High Seat and Man reveal the powerful presence of the massive Dodds and Helvellyn which, when clad in winter snows, seem to take on Alpine proportion. On return, the descent by the shoulder of Ashness Fell presents awesome views over Derwentwater.

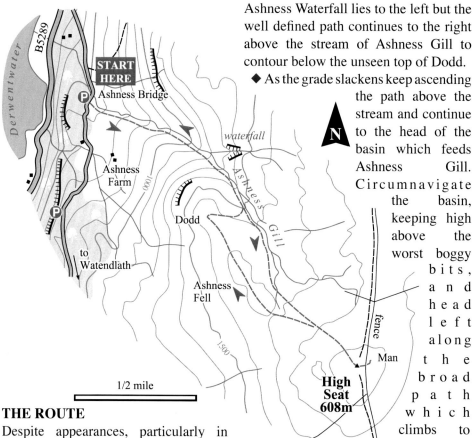

Ashness Waterfall lies to the left but the well defined path continues to the right above the stream of Ashness Gill to contour below the unseen top of Dodd.

◆ As the grade slackens keep ascending the path above the stream and continue to the head of the basin which feeds Ashness Gill. Circumnavigate the basin, keeping high above the worst boggy bits, and head left along the broad path which climbs to the Trig Point and summit of High Seat. For even closer views to the Thirlmere Valley and the mighty chain of The Dodds and Helvellyn, cross the dip and wire fence heading east to the rocky top known as Man (reached in 100m).

◆ Return to the head of the basin then climb left (west). Various paths lead to the shoulder and cairned tops of

THE ROUTE

Despite appearances, particularly in wintry conditions, this walk shouldn't be underestimated – in execution it always seems longer than expected! From the car park go left descending the road until just before Ashness Bridge a path ascends to the right to pass the stone hut. Climb the well defined path to the right of Barrow Beck. Once the fell wall is passed the way steepens.

WALK 9

The top called Man with the snow clad Dodds seen beyond

Ashness Gill running to
Ashness Bridge

View from
Ashness Fell

Ashness Fell which offer fine views over
Borrowdale and Derwentwater. Descend
the heathery shoulder to the final cairned
top known as Dodd. Go right back down
to the original path traversing just above
Ashness Gill.

FACT SHEET
CLASS: Intermediate Fell Walk
(alt 608m).
LENGTH: 4¾ km.
TIME: 3 hours.
DIFFICULTY: Difficult, with some
strenuous ascent (460m).
START & FINISH: Ashness Bridge Car
Park in Strutta Wood (269 196).
MAPS: OS L89 or OL4.
HOSTELRIES: High Lodore Farm
(Shepherd's Café) and Caffle House
Tearoom in Watendlath are nearby.

WALK 10
SURPRISE VIEW, ASHNESS BRIDGE, DERWENTWATER AND LODORE FALLS

If you want a walk for all seasons, a world class landscape, breathtaking beauty, variety and interest, then take this walk which traverses above, and below, the wooded heights of Lodore. Starting from Surprise View it makes an anticlockwise round first following the Watendlath Road to Ashness Bridge before dropping to Barrow Bay. A walk along Derwentwater's shoreline then leads to Kettlewell Car Park and Lodore Woods before ascent, beside Lodore Falls on neglected and tree bestrewn pathways, climbs back to the heights.

THE ROUTE

Surprise View, opposite the car park, is quite stunning. Descend the Watendlath Road to cross Ashness Bridge (850m). Beyond the bridge take the path rising to the right.

Pass through the wall, then bear down to the left following the narrow path. Open at first, the path drops into trees before steepening and descending to a level terrace. Take the acute fork left and descend the stony path to gain the Watendlath Road. Go down the road and at the bottom cross the Borrowdale Road, then go down the steps to Barrow Bay Landing Stage.

◆ Head left and take the path beside the shoreline (if flooded follow the road) which leads (in 950m) to Kettlewell Car Park. Cross the road and take the gap in the stone wall to follow the path rightwards through the woods. Beyond Mary Mount Hotel, located on the opposite side of the road, bear left away from the road. Continue until a stony path moves off to the left, just before a descent leads to the footbridge above the Lodore Hotel, and make a slight climb to a terrace, with bench, located at the base of the Lodore Falls.

Barrow Bay

B5289

Ashness Bridge

Kettlewell Car Park

Mary Mount

Ashness Farm

Surprise View

Lodore Hotel

Lodore Falls

START HERE

Gowder Crag

Shepherd's Cafe

to Watendlath

1/2 mile

Looking north from Surprise View

Unfortunately the falls are now obscured by trees.

◆ Climb the path leading up by the falls. The object is to reach the base of the cliff known as Gowder Crag which rises out of the woods above. A terraced path leads first left and then back right but is now rather overgrown and the fork right is easily missed. Most make direct ascent, though steep, stony and unpleasant, directly to the foot of the crag. From here follow the terraced path rightwards, negotiating fallen trees, taking a high line above the falls. Near the top of the falls a path leads up left to cross a fenceline and old wall. Continue until the path makes slight descent to the wide hairpin bend in Watendlath Beck at the old ford.

◆ Just upstream of the ford a narrow path makes diagonal ascent through the woods, rising to intercept a larger path. Go left along the level terrace until an ancient trackway rises to the right. Ascend the trackway until it intercepts a further broader track. Go left and follow the main track which finally rejoins the surfaced Watendlath Road. Bear left along the road to the car park.

FACT SHEET
CLASS: Low Fell Walk (alt 250m).
LENGTH: 5½ km.
TIME: 3½ hours.
DIFFICULTY: Mildly difficult, short road sections and a short strenuous ascent by Lodore Falls (160m).
START & FINISH: Surprise View Car Park in Ashness Wood (268 190).
MAPS: OS L89 or OL4.
HOSTELRIES: Mary Mount Hotel enroute. High Lodore Farm (Shepherd's Café) and Caffle House Tearoom in Watendlath are nearby.

WALK 11
DERWENTWATER HEIGHTS - BY CASTLERIGG TO WALLA CRAG

At the end of Borrowdale the northern head of Derwentwater opens to Keswick and the Northern Fells to stunning effect. Savouring the myriad of tree fringed delights of the lake and exploring the countryside beyond, this clockwise round rising to Walla Crag offers a wonderful panorama of the surrounding fells.

THE ROUTE

Opposite the landing stages at Derwent Head take the path left into Cockshott Wood. Follow through the wood to exit following a lane which leads across the fields. Cross the road and climb the steps into Castlehead Wood. Follow the main path ascending steeply through the woods until a path climbs to the right to crest the rocky knoll of Castle Head.

◆ Return to the main path then bear right and descend. Continue rightwards until a kissing gate leads to a lane across the field. Gain Springs Road and bear right, ascending to cross a bridge opposite Springs Farm. Take the track up through the wood. Go right at the junction then follow up the right edge

FACT SHEET
CLASS: *Intermediate Fell Walk (alt 379m).*
LENGTH: *8½ km.*
TIME: *3½ hours.*
DIFFICULTY: *Mildly difficult, with steep ascent (300m) and descent.*
START & FINISH: *Derwent Head Car Park (264 229).*
MAPS: *OS L89 or OL4.*
HOSTELRIES: *Theatre by the Lake Café and cafes enroute by Derwent Head.*

of the wood. Continue in ascent until a footbridge crosses left to Castlerigg Road. Bear right and continue to its end to re-cross the stream by a footbridge. The path leads up by the wall, crosses a stile, and out onto the open shoulder of the fell. Ascend the steep grassy nose.

Over Strand-shag Bay to Walla Crag, left.

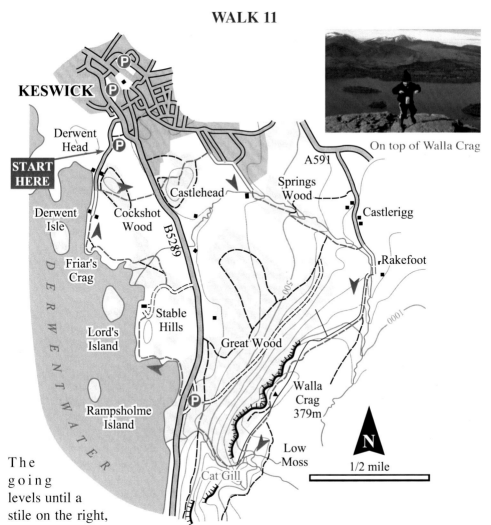

KESWICK

Derwent Head

START HERE

A591

Springs Wood

Castlehead

Castlerigg

Derwent Isle

Cockshot Wood

B5289

Friar's Crag

Rakefoot

DERWENT WATER

Stable Hills

Lord's Island

Great Wood

500

1000

Rampsholme Island

Walla Crag 379m

Low Moss

Cat Gill

On top of Walla Crag

N

1/2 mile

The going levels until a stile on the right, over the fence, leads to a path which follows the edge of the crag. Those wishing to stay away from the cliff edge may take a higher stile. Follow the path which crosses the head of a gully to climb onto the polished rock cap of Walla Crag. Stunning views.

◆ Return to the boundary wall and go right (south) to follow down the shoulder. Continue down the rocky path making steep descent above the tumbling waters of Cat Gill to meet a track by a bridge. Bear right into Great Wood. Follow the stony track until a descent leads into the car park. Pass straight across to find a path which descends to a gap in the wall by the Borrowdale Road. Cross the road and take the gap in the wall opposite to follow the path to the lakeshore.

◆ Bear right following around Calfclose Bay and by Stable Hills until a path forks off left into the wood of The Ings. Keep along the path to pass Strandshag Bay to the stand of Scots Pine on Friar's Crag. Continue easily back to Derwent Head.

WALK 12
THE ROUND OF DERWENTWATER

A classic outing providing easy walking amongst stunning scenery. Overlooked on all sides by high fells, fringed by wonderful natural woods, this is the perfect walk to experience the myriad moods and many facets of lovely Derwentwater. An anticlockwise circumnavigation of the lake with the first leg, Keswick to Nichol End, taken by Kesick Launch. There are a further five Landing Stages around the lake and the walk can be shortened if desired by hopping on a launch.

THE ROUTE

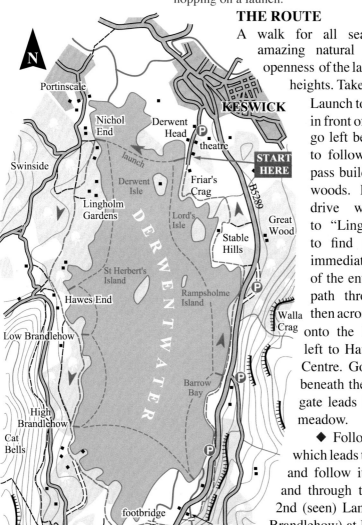

A walk for all seasons contrasting amazing natural woods with the openness of the lake and views to the heights. Take the anticlockwise Launch to Nichol End. Pass in front of Marina Café then go left behind the building to follow a wide track to pass buildings and through woods. Emerge onto the drive which leads left to "Lingholm – Private" to find a gate and path immediately to the right of the entrance. Follow the path through woods and then across a field to emerge onto the lane which leads left to Hawse End Outdoor Centre. Go left on the lane beneath the buildings until a gate leads left into the open meadow.

◆ Follow the broad path which leads to the water's edge and follow it, beside the lake and through the woods, to the 2nd (seen) Landing Stage (High Brandlehow) at Brandlehowe Bay. Continue to pass the old copper mine spoil and pass the buildings until at the last building, on the edge of Manesty Wood, a path leads off left

1 mile

Myrtle Bay

Angling for char

back to the lakeside. Follow the path to emerge into open ground and bear left, walkway in places, to traverse the head of the lake and cross a footbridge over the River Derwent. Continue on the path to gain the gate/stile leading onto the main Borrowdale road (this section can be underwater in times of flood).

◆ Head left along the narrow pavement until, on passing the Public Conveniences, a signed permissive footpath leads right across the road to follow behind the Lodore Falls Hotel. Cross the beck by a little metal footbridge and follow the path, initially running just above the stone wall, up and around to the left through Lodore Wood. The path soon reaches the roadside, Mary Mount Hotel opposite, and follows through the woods to the right of the road. At Kettlewell Car Park the way crosses the road then bears right along a raised promenade above the lake. At its end, go left and keep to the path which rounds the promontory to arrive at Barrow Bay. Pass the landing stage of Ashness Gate and continue along the shoreline to find the wide main path, from the road, which leads on through the woods. If the

shoreline is flooded then the road lies just above.

◆ Follow the path around Calfclose Bay and exit the Yew Wood to gain the path running along the edge of the open field. Pass the buildings of Stable Hills and follow the lane until the path drops leftwards to a gate. Pass through the gate and follow along the track through the wood of The Ings. Round Strandshag Bay and continue to pass the tree bedecked headland of Friar's Crag to gain the surfaced track leading back to the landing stages and Derwent Head.

FACT SHEET
CLASS: *Valley Walk (alt 75m).*
LENGTH: 12 km.
TIME: 4 hours.
DIFFICULTY: Easy; level paths and tracks prevail though cumulatively there is 330m of ascent.
START & FINISH: Derwent Head Car Park (264 229). Take the anticlockwise 1st stage Keswick Launch to Nichol End (cheap and dogs are free).
MAPS: OS L89 or OL4.
HOSTELRIES: Cafés at Derwent Head, Nichol End and near the south end of the lake is Shepherd's Cafe. Lodore Falls and Mary Mount Hotels found enroute.

WALK 13
OVER CATBELLS RETURNING BY DERWENTWATER

Running above the western shore of Derwentwater, in full view of Keswick, the evocative curvature of Skelgill Bank and the domed head of Catbells proves irresistible to many. Indeed Catbells offers wonderful position and outstanding views. Tackled in this manner, making an anticlockwise circuit, returning through Manesty Woods and along the shore of Derwentwater, this is an outing of excellence.

THE ROUTE

Take the stone steps which rise from the car park, and follow the well worn path, over littered fragments and polished outcrops of grey Skiddaw Slate, to make steep ascent of Skelgill Bank. Continue along the level ridge, to cross the workings of the ancient Brandlehow copper mine which has risen all the way from the lake shore far below. The ridge dips down to a col beneath the final pyramid of Catbells. Make steep ascent to gain the polished rock dome summit of Catbells and enjoy the superb and extensive view; particularly outstanding over the Newlands valley to the North Western Fells and over Derwentwater and its emerald isles to Skiddaw and Blencathra beyond Keswick.

◆ Continue along the shoulder and descend to Hause Gate from where a path leads off down to the left. Descend the path, with a steep stepped section near the top, until the path bears right across the hillside and the going eases. Follow the path rightwards, diagonally down the hillside until, at an acute bend, with the main path heading off to the left, a path to the right is followed and will be found to lead down to a gate. Beyond the gate a path drops off down to the left, to skirt the oak wood, to gain the surfaced road. This section can be muddy when wet.

◆ Bear left until a cattle grid on the right leads into Manesty Woods. Follow a surfaced track until the lake can be seen. Go right and keep low to gain the footpath, by the lakeshore, which leads around Brandelhow Bay. Continue along the path to pass the landing stage of High Brandelhow and Withesike and Victoria Bays. Continue to the large wooden hand in the woods just before Victoria Bay and on to the landing stage of Low Brandelhow. The path/track then bears away from the lake to pass beneath the buildings of Hawes End Outdoor Pursuits Centre. Continue until a track rises to the left and take this to climb to the road and ascend to regain the car park.

FACT SHEET
CLASS: Intermediate Fell Walk
(alt 451m).
LENGTH: 7 km.
TIME: 3½ hours.
DIFFICULTY: Difficult; steep ascent up Skelgill Bank and Cat Bells (465m).
START & FINISH: Hawes End car park (NY 247 212)
MAPS: OS L89 or OL4.
HOSTELRIES: Nothing enroute, Swinside Inn nearby.

Catbells from Skelgill Bank

WALK 13

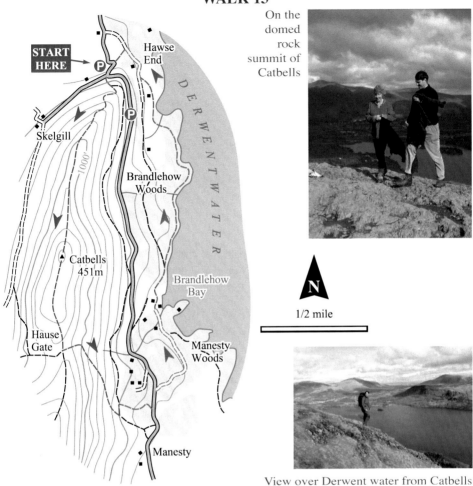

START
HERE

Hawse
End

Skelgill

1000'

Brandlehow
Woods

Catbells
451m

Brandlehow
Bay

Hause
Gate

Manesty
Woods

Manesty

D E R W E N T W A T E R

On the
domed
rock
summit of
Catbells

N

1/2 mile

View over Derwent water from Catbells

Over
Derwent
Isle
to the
shapely
dome of
Catbells

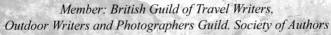

WALK 14
A ROUND OF THE NEWLANDS VALLEY

Running between Borrowdale and Buttermere, set deep in the North Western Fells, the Newlands Valley was once the hub of extensive mining activity. Today, remote from the more popular tourist centres, it is now a haven of calm and quiet. This clockwise route, traversing its three heads and crossing the body of the valley to pass through Little Town the fabled home of Mrs Tiggy-Winkle, savours much of its rich and magical mountain atmosphere.

THE ROUTE

Ascend the road in the direction of Little Town then go right over the stile and up the steps to gain the track which leads towards the head of the valley. Bear right along the track and continue until, at the end

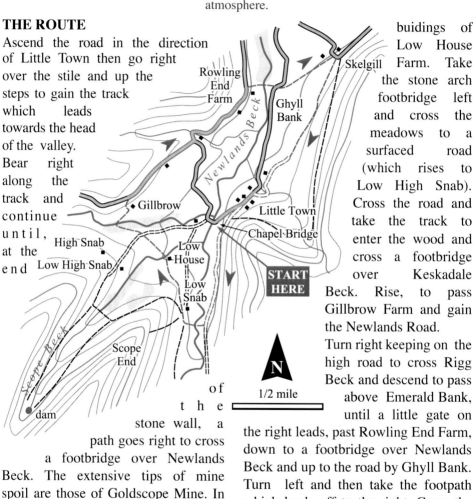

buidings of Low House Skelgill Farm. Take the stone arch footbridge left and cross the meadows to a surfaced road (which rises to Low High Snab). Cross the road and take the track to enter the wood and cross a footbridge over Keskadale Beck. Rise, to pass Gillbrow Farm and gain the Newlands Road. Turn right keeping on the high road to cross Rigg Beck and descend to pass above Emerald Bank, until a little gate on the right leads, past Rowling End Farm, down to a footbridge over Newlands Beck and up to the road by Ghyll Bank. Turn left and then take the footpath which leads off to the right. Cross the fields to pass through the hamlet of Skelgill. Go right, up the road, then right again between the house and barns of Skelgill Farm. A grassy path leads through the fields rising slightly, with wonderful views to the surrounding

of the stone wall, a path goes right to cross a footbridge over Newlands Beck. The extensive tips of mine spoil are those of Goldscope Mine. In Elizabethan times sufficient gold was extracted from the copper for the mine to be claimed by the Crown.

◆ Bear right along the track to traverse above the building of Low Snab. Follow the grassy track which falls to round the

Towards the head of Newlands

Stone bridge leading to meadows behind Low House Farm

Little Town - fabled home of Mrs Tiggy- Winkle

FACT SHEET
CLASS: *Valley Walk (alt 230m).*
LENGTH: 7½ km.
TIME: 3 hours.
DIFFICULTY: Easy; excellent paths and tracks with 250m of ascent overall.
START & FINISH: Limited parking by Chapel Bridge (231 194).
MAPS: OS L89 or OL4.
HOSTELRIES: Tea Room at Little Town, Swinside Inn nearby.

fells, then falling to pass the isolated East House. Continue on the lane, over a narrow footbridge, to emerge onto a surfaced road. Turn left and pass through Little Town, the fabled home of Beatrix Potter's Lucie and Mrs Tiggy-Winkle, to descend the hill to Chapel Bridge.

WALK 15
LATRIGG ABOVE KESWICK

Little Latrigg stands large above Keswick to offer fine views. Although an outlier of the greater Skiddaw Massif it occupies a dominant position and is a worthy independent top. This route makes steep ascent to the summit from Spooney Green Lane before descending the gentle eastern shoulder. Finally the route traverses west across the face of the fell along a delightfully secretive track and path.

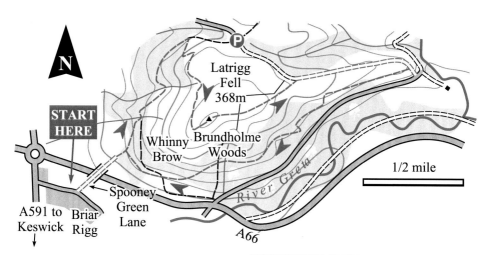

THE ROUTE

Those who think they know Latrigg by casual observation from Keswick will be pleasantly surprised by the hidden interest of this route. Climb Spooney Green Lane taking the bridge over the A66. Continue to pass the woods beneath Whinney Brow. Follow the track in ascent, to pass Ewe How, Round How and Birkett Wood, until, with forestry below, a green track zigzags off to the right. Ascend this until the track bears off right at an old stone gatestoop. Making gentle ascent, traverse the hillside to gain a bench and very fine position above Keswick town. Derwent Water and Borrowdale lie beyond. Skiddaw rises majestically behind. The Dodds and Helvellyn stretch to the east.

◆ A grassy track climbs the shoulder to the highest point of Latrigg Fell and continues along by the raised bank which runs along the rim of the hill. Cross the stile before descending slightly leftwards down the broad shoulder to gain a track above the wood. Follow the track until, at a point where it steepens before it falls to intercept

FACT SHEET
CLASS: *Intermediate Fell Walk (alt 368m).*
LENGTH: *8½ km.*
TIME: *3 hours.*
DIFFICULTY: *Mildly difficult; with steep ascent (440m) and easier descent.*
START & FINISH: *Briar Rigg, edge of Keswick, parking by road (267 241).*
MAPS: *OS L89 or OL4.*
HOSTELRIES: *Nothing enroute, plentiful in Keswick.*

Latrigg, left, rising above the River Greta as it flows through Keswick

a surfaced road, a grassy track signed 'Permitted Woodland Walk Keswick' leads sharply off right.

◆ Take this track, traversing above the trees of Brundholme Wood. Continue along the path, dropping down into the woods for a short way before climbing again to follow a lesser track. Continue along the track, there are a number of undulations, to traverse the thickly wooded hillside finally to emerge into the open beneath Whinney Brow. Large sweet-chestnut trees and Scots pine above. Keep right at the junction and then descend left to cross a track and intercept a further track at a lower level. Follow this to the right to emerge by gate onto Spooney Green Lane.

Traversing Latrigg with Skiddaw behind

Looking east to Clough Head and Great Dodd

WALK 16
KESWICK'S GRETA GORGE

The climb through the oaks and broad leaved trees of Brundholme Woods, with occasional views down to the river, is quite delightful and at its most colourful in Autumn. Return is made along the old railway line which traverses the bottom of the gorge. Now quiet, with the rails long gone, it makes for a fascinating journey beside the river and deep in the trees with views from the bridges revealing the full power of the River Greta.

THE ROUTE

From the Moot Hall walk down the square to cross the main road and continue down the right side pavement. Turn right up Stanger St and follow it to its end by the river. Go right and then left over the footbridge to enter Fitz Park. Bear right and leave the park taking the steps near the Museum. Turn left along the road and left again to cross in front of the swimming pool. Pass the end of the pool to enter the old station car park.

◆ Turn right until, a little way alongside the old platform, an opening leads off down to the left. Bear right to find a narrow stile leading onto the road. Proceed down the road until, just before the old railway bridge, a road branches off left (signed 'Public Footpath Windebrowe'). Follow this through the trees and go left at the next junction. Exit through the gate of Brundholme Country House Hotel and bear right to follow the road over Windebrowe.

◆ A signed gate 'Footpath Brundholme Woods' leads down to the right. Descend steps to a track. Keep down the track to the River Greta and the old stone bridge (1817). Continue along the path above the river. With impressive views to the river, steep drops in places, follow the path through the woods and pass beneath the A66 concrete road bridge. Continue along the path above the river, through Brundholme Woods, until it climbs (with a field to the right),

The return route crosses the old railway bridges which span the River Greta, with Brundholme Woods beyond

WALK 16

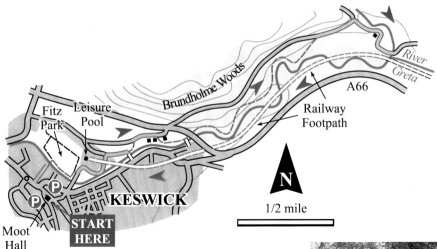

KESWICK

Fitz Park

Leisure Pool

Brundholme Woods

Railway Footpath

A66

River Greta

N

1/2 mile

Moot Hall

START HERE

Old and new bridges spanning the the River Greta through Greta Gorge

Return is made along the old railway line built in 1865 and closed in 1972

to gain the surfaced road. Bear right and follow the road until a track leads down right, with the tree lined gorge of Glenderaterra Beck down below to the left, to pass Brundholme Farm. Gain the line of the old railway in the valley bottom and bear right, following it with considerable interest and a slight climb up to pass under the the new road bridge, back to the old station.

FACT SHEET
CLASS: *Valley Walk (alt 185m).*
LENGTH: 9½ km.
TIME: 3 hours.
DIFFICULTY: Mildly difficult; overall there is 290m of ascent, though return along the line of the old railway is mainly level.
START & FINISH: Moot Hall centre of Keswick (266 234). Main car parks nearby.
MAPS: OS L89 or OL4.
HOSTELRIES: Plentiful in Keswick.

WALK 17
CASTLERIGG STONE CIRCLE TO TEWET TARN

Stunningly situated amongst the fells, Castlerigg Stone Circle is arguably the most impressive in Cumbria. Tewet is an old name for a Peewit/Lapwing/Green Plover. After visiting the circle this walk makes an anticlockwise round crossing the Naddle Valley before rising to the low shoulder of Naddle Fell. From here descent leads to St John's Church and is followed by a traverse over Low Naddle Fell to Tewet Tarn. A quiet road section gains the fields below Goosewell Farm and slight ascent joins the circle.

THE ROUTE

There is a timelessly impressive backdrop to this walk whichever way you turn. Mighty Blencathra and Skiddaw to the north, Grisedale Pike and the north western fells to the west, Castlerigg Fell to the south and The Dodds and Helvellyn to the east. The Neolithic stone circle of Castlerigg (circa 2,500 BC) could hardly fail to make a huge impression. A little gate leads to the circle and a viewpoint east over Naddle Valley. Return to the road,

bear right, then right again in 200m to follow the path across the fields to the house known as High Nest. Pass through the buildings and down the lane until, at a cattle grid, the path bears off left to join a lower lane. Go right to the main road joining it on Nest Brow hill. Keep left to find a stile through the wall in 50m.

◆ Follow the path down through the fields. Cross a little bridge and bear left in the valley bottom. Cross the gated bridge over the clear waters of Naddle

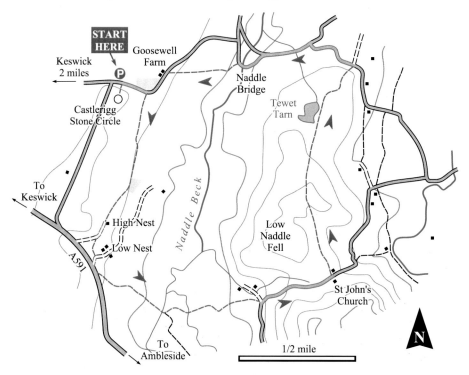

Castlerigg Stone Circle with Blencathra beyond

Beck, continuing past a little wood to bear right across a field. After a way, a sign points left and this is followed to a kissing gate which leads to rougher fellside. The path leads to an exit onto a stony track. Continue over the brow of the hill to little St John's Church. Rebuilt 1845 and little changed since, it gives its name to the next vale below. The stile opposite leads to a path beneath a crag and over a stone wall to cross Low Naddle Fell. Descent passes east of forlorn Tewet Tarn to join the road (old A66). Go left and left again at the junction (older A66) to cross Naddle Bridge. A path leads left off the road. At the divergence of ways go left through a gate to make a diagonal crossing over the field, ascending gently (right of way though poorly defined) directly to Goosewell Farm. Bear left up the road.

Tewet Tarn with Blencathra behind

Pass to St John's Church

FACT SHEET
CLASS: *Low Fell Walk (alt 250m).*
LENGTH: *7 km.*
TIME: *2½ hours.*
DIFFICULTY: *Mildly difficult; with 210m of ascent.*
START & FINISH: *Parking opposite Castlerigg Stone Circle (291 237)*
MAPS: *OS L89 or OL4.*
HOSTELRIES: *None enroute.*

WALK 18
SKIDDAW

Skiddaw is the 3rd highest mountain massif in the Lake District and its summit, High Man, is much prized. Though ascent and descent by this route is a relatively straightforward matter, if somewhat strenuous, the extensive and wonderful views make up for any lack of adventure. In descent a small extension also includes the top of Little Man.

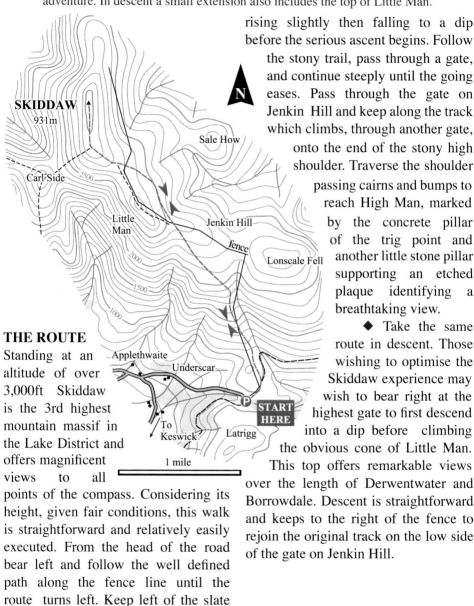

rising slightly then falling to a dip before the serious ascent begins. Follow the stony trail, pass through a gate, and continue steeply until the going eases. Pass through the gate on Jenkin Hill and keep along the track which climbs, through another gate, onto the end of the stony high shoulder. Traverse the shoulder passing cairns and bumps to reach High Man, marked by the concrete pillar of the trig point and another little stone pillar supporting an etched plaque identifying a breathtaking view.

◆ Take the same route in descent. Those wishing to optimise the Skiddaw experience may wish to bear right at the highest gate to first descend into a dip before climbing the obvious cone of Little Man. This top offers remarkable views over the length of Derwentwater and Borrowdale. Descent is straightforward and keeps to the right of the fence to rejoin the original track on the low side of the gate on Jenkin Hill.

THE ROUTE

Standing at an altitude of over 3,000ft Skiddaw is the 3rd highest mountain massif in the Lake District and offers magnificent views to all points of the compass. Considering its height, given fair conditions, this walk is straightforward and relatively easily executed. From the head of the road bear left and follow the well defined path along the fence line until the route turns left. Keep left of the slate Shepherd's Cross and follow the well defined broad path along the shoulder

WALK 18

Skiddaw high above Derwentwater and Keswick

The summit of Skiddaw

Looking over mist filled Borrowdale from
the path rising to Skiddaw

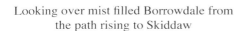

FACT SHEET
CLASS: High Fell Walk (alt 931m).
LENGTH: 5 km.
TIME: 3 hours.
*DIFFICULTY: Difficult; with 650m of
straightforward ascent.*
*START & FINISH: Parking at the head
of the Applethwaite road behind Latrigg
(260 253)*
MAPS: OS L89 or OL4.
HOSTELRIES: None enroute.

WALK 19
GRISEDALE PIKE

Ascent of the long and aesthetic east ridge is the most popular way to gain the summit of pyramidal Grisedale Pike. Beyond the summit this route traverses to Hobcarton Head before descending to Coledale Hause. Return is made by following the old mining track, which first descends into the head of Coledale to the south of Force Crag, and then continues along the north side of the valley.

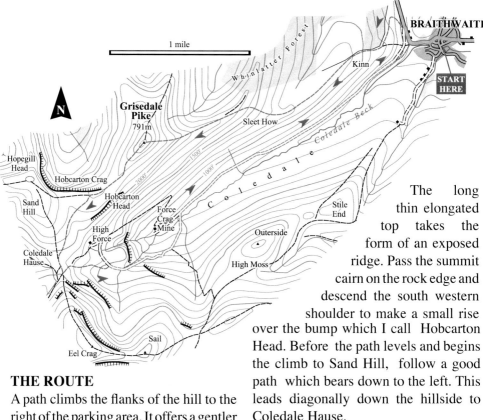

The long thin elongated top takes the form of an exposed ridge. Pass the summit cairn on the rock edge and descend the south western shoulder to make a small rise over the bump which I call Hobcarton Head. Before the path levels and begins the climb to Sand Hill, follow a good path which bears down to the left. This leads diagonally down the hillside to Coledale Hause.

◆ Below lies the upper basin of Coledale with High Force waterfall plunging into it. Don't be tempted to enter. Between it and Coledale lies the great precipice of Force Crag. From the crossroads of Coldedale Hause follow the distinct path which takes the southern edge of the basin. This picks up a mine track and leads safely past Force Crag down to cross Coledale Beck below

THE ROUTE

A path climbs the flanks of the hill to the right of the parking area. It offers a gentler approach than the more direct route which climbs from the elbow in the bend of the road below. Once the shoulder is gained it gives straightforward ascent over the gentle top of Kinn. Pass the natural spring of Lanty Well to the left. Steeper ground leads to the shoulder of Sleet How. The final section of the east ridge steepens to climb the pyramidal head of Grisedale Pike.

Grisedale Pike seen above the foot of Derwentwater

the mine buildings. A wild and desolate location. A great waterfall, Low Force, plunges down Force Crag. Easy return is made directly down Coledale via the mine track.

Looking to the head of Coledale

Grisedale Pike's East Ridge

FACT SHEET
CLASS: High Fell Walk (alt 791m).
LENGTH: 10¾ km.
TIME: 4½ hours.
DIFFICULTY: Very Difficult; on good paths, though exposed to the elements (735m of ascent).
START & FINISH: Small car park above Braithwaite (NY 277 237).
MAPS: OS L89 or OL4.
HOSTELRIES: Coledale Inn and Middle Ruddings Inn, Braithwaite.

WALK 20
DODD WOOD, BASSENTHWAITE LAKE AND ST BEGA'S

A fascinating anticlockwise round leads through Dodd Wood and over the fell known as Watches before descent leads to a crossing of the meadows to gain the shores of Bassenthwaite Lake. Scenic return via Scarness Bay, Broadness, Bowness Bay and over the meadows to the ancient site of St Bega's Church ends by walking passed the grand house and gardens of Mirehouse.

THE ROUTE

Cross the footbridge above the tea room and go first left and then right to ascend a grassy track through the tall pines. Turn left along the high track. It narrows and drops to intercept a track rising from below. Keep right and make steep ascent to gain the open fell. Bear left. At the corner of the fence climb to gain the high shoulder then traverse left to the cairned summit of Watches. (Alternatively make a level traverse above the fell wall). Descend the nose by a path to the little wooden gate in the wall. Pass through the gate and descend the path running alongside the wall to a little hollow. Go left along the grassy track and pass through the stone wall before bearing right to descend the field to a junction with a track. Go left and pass through the gate to gain the surfaced road. Bear left until, at the bottom of the hill and junction with A591, a signed path directly opposite the buildings of High Side is taken. Descend the field to its corner and bear right down a long narrow field to continue through fields to the buildings of Mire Side. Go left between the buildings and exit to the right (signed Scarness). Follow across the field (ill defined path) with a hedge to the right. Exit onto a road and cross it to a cattle grid and concrete track opposite. Follow down this and

FACT SHEET
CLASS: Low Fell Walk (alt 333m).
LENGTH: 11 km.
TIME: 4 hours.
DIFFICULTY: Difficult; a longish outing with a steep climb (avoidable) to the top of Watches. Overall there is 370m of ascent.
START & FINISH: : Dodd Wood Car Park beneath the Old Sawmill Tearoom (235 281).
MAPS: OS L89 or OL4.
HOSTELRIES: Old Sawmill Tearoom.

through the gate to enter the property of Scarness. Walk across the lawn (public footpath!) to the left of the house and join the drive to follow it leftward to exit onto the road.

◆ Turn left then right down an overgrown path, 'Holiday Park' to the right, to gain a little gate and path leading left to the lakeshore (National Nature Reserve). Follow the path round the headland between Scarness and Bowness Bay and continue to regain the road. Bear right along the tree lined road until, within a wood, a path bears off to the right. Cross the fields and little wood to gain the lane leading to St Bega's Church.

◆ Go right then take the track off left before the church. This track leads to the right of Mirehouse and back to the A591. Whilst staying at Mirehouse, Tennyson took his inspiration to write

WALK 20

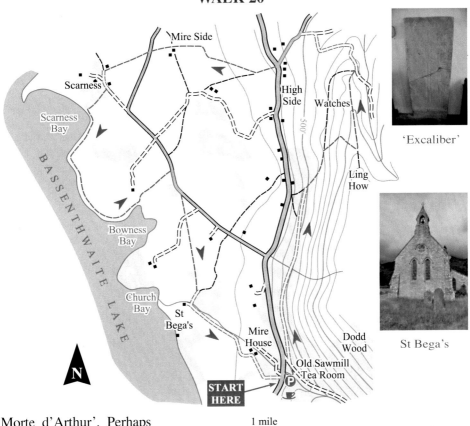

'Excaliber'

St Bega's

'Morte d'Arthur'. Perhaps the sword depicted on an ancient gravestone within St Bega's became Excaliber?

1 mile

Dodd Wood

Bowness Bay

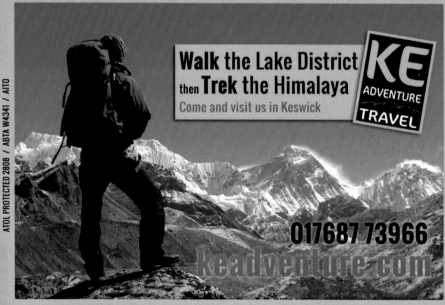